IF I HIT AT SCHOOL

A Story That Teach Kids How to Stop Hitting Others

David Fletcher

Copyright

THIS
book belongs to

NAME:

⬦ - ⬦

AGE:

⬦ - ⬦

HITTING IS WHEN I TRY TO HURT SOMEONE.

Circle the feelings you have when you hit someone

HURTING OR TRYING TO HURT SOMEONE IS NEVER OK.

IT IS AGAINST THE SCHOOL RULES.

IF I HIT SOMEONE AT SCHOOL I WILL GET INTO TROUBLE.

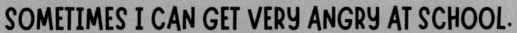

SOMETIMES I CAN GET VERY ANGRY AT SCHOOL.

IT IS NEVER OK TO HIT SOMEONE BECAUSE
I AM ANGRY.

ADULTS MAY BE VERY CROSS WITH ME AND
I MAY GET CONSEQUENCES I DON'T LIKE.

IF I FEEL ANGRY I CAN TRY:

WALKING AWAY

TELLING AN ADULT

DOING A CALMING ACTIVITY

LIKE PAINTING OR DRAWING.

READING.

PLAYING WITH FRIENDS

OR DO OTHER THINGS THAT CAN CALM
ME DOWN.

FINDING A FRIEND TO TALK TO

WRITING DOWN WHAT MADE ME ANGRY

IT IS NEVER OK TO HIT SOMEONE.

IF I GET ANGRY I CAN TRY TO STAY
CALM AND FOLLOW SCHOOL RULES.

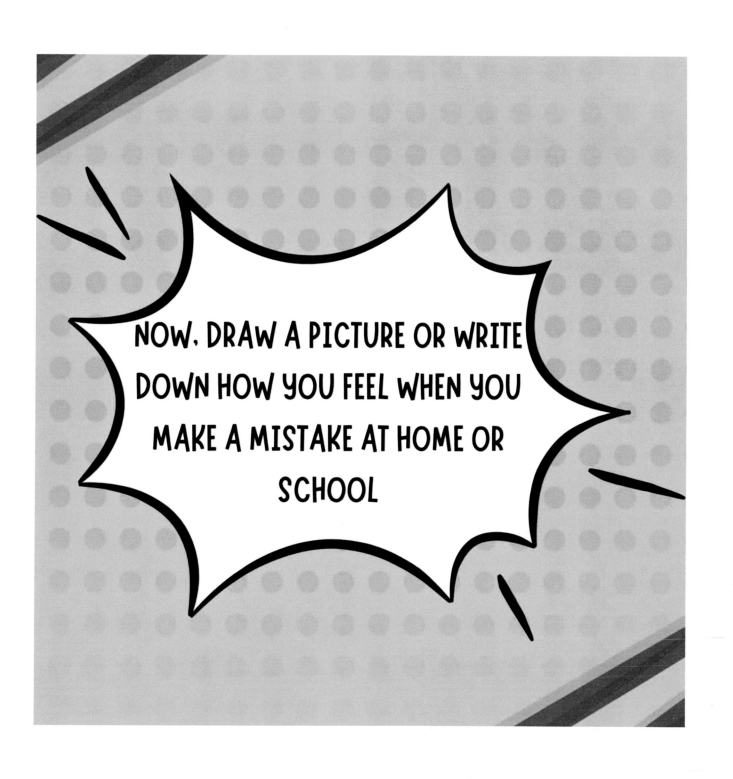

NOTES

NOTES

Other Social Stories by David Fletcher

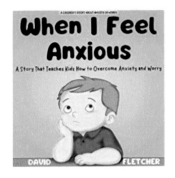

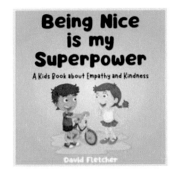

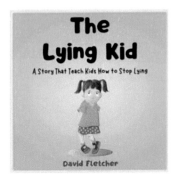

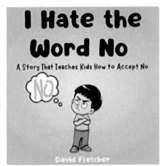

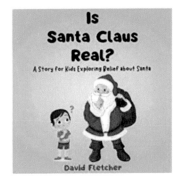

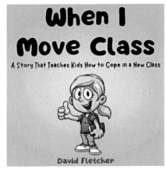

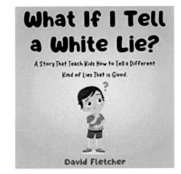

Other Social Stories by David Fletcher

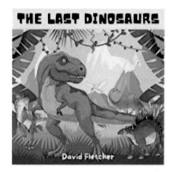

Get Them on Amazon!

Made in the USA
Las Vegas, NV
01 October 2023

78356450R00019